First World War
and Army of Occupation
War Diary
France, Belgium and Germany

52 DIVISION
Divisional Troops
Divisional Signal Company
1 April 1918 - 27 May 1919

WO95/2893/4

The Naval & Military Press Ltd
www.nmarchive.com
Published in association with The National Archives

Published by

The Naval & Military Press Ltd

Unit 10 Ridgewood Industrial Park,

Uckfield, East Sussex,

TN22 5QE England

Tel: +44 (0) 1825 749494

www.naval-military-press.com

www.nmarchive.com

This diary has been reprinted in facsimile from the original. Any imperfections are inevitably reproduced and the quality may fall short of modern type and cartographic standards.

© **Crown Copyright**
Images reproduced by permission of The National Archives, London, England, 2015.

Contents

Document type	Place/Title	Date From	Date To
Heading	WO95/2893-4		
Heading	52nd Division 52nd Divl Signal Coy R.E. Apr 1918-May 1919		
Heading	52nd Divisional Engineers Disembarked Marseilles From Egypt 17.4.18 52nd Divisional Signal Company R.E. April 1918		
War Diary	Jaffa Ludd	01/04/1918	06/04/1918
War Diary	Kantara	07/04/1918	08/04/1918
War Diary	Alexandria	11/04/1918	11/04/1918
War Diary	Marseilles	17/04/1918	18/04/1918
War Diary	Rue	21/04/1918	28/04/1918
War Diary	Aire	29/04/1918	30/04/1918
Diagram etc	Diagram Of Communications		
Miscellaneous	D.A.G. 3rd Echelon	26/05/1918	26/05/1918
Miscellaneous	Royal Engineers		
Heading	War Diary 52nd (Lowland) Divisional Signal Coy R.E. From 1st May 1918 To 31st May 1918 Volume XXXVI		
War Diary	Aire	01/05/1918	06/05/1918
War Diary	Chateau D'Acq	07/05/1918	30/05/1918
Diagram etc	52nd Divl Signal Coy Diagram Of Communications		
Heading	War Diary 52nd Divisional Signal Coy R.E. From 1st June 1918 To 30th June 1918 Volume XXXVII		
War Diary		01/06/1918	30/06/1918
War Diary	Chateau D'Acq	08/06/1918	23/06/1918
Heading	War Diary 52nd Divnl Signal Coy From 1st July 1918 To 31st July 1918 Volume XXXVIII With Appendices 1 and 2		
War Diary	Chateau D'Acq	02/07/1918	23/07/1918
War Diary	Pernes	30/07/1918	31/07/1918
Diagram etc	52 Division Circulation Diagram		
War Diary	Pernes	02/08/1918	02/08/1918
War Diary	Maroeuil	14/08/1918	16/08/1918
War Diary	Villers Chatel	20/08/1918	21/08/1918
War Diary	Hermaville	22/08/1918	22/08/1918
War Diary	Bretencourt	23/08/1918	24/08/1918
War Diary	Blaireville Quarry	24/08/1918	31/08/1918
Diagram etc	Diagram		
Miscellaneous	Signal Communications During Operations	24/08/1918	24/08/1918
Heading	War Diary 52nd (Lowland) Divisional Signal From 1/9/18 To 30/9/18 Volume XL With Appendices 1 To 6		
War Diary	Croisilles	01/09/1918	17/09/1918
War Diary	Queant	19/09/1918	30/09/1918
Diagram etc	Diagram		
Diagram etc	Diagram Of Infy Lines Wireless & Visual		
Diagram etc	Diagram		
Map	Map		
Miscellaneous	Appendix "D" To 52nd Division Order No. 136	25/09/1918	25/09/1918
Map	Map		
Miscellaneous	Report On Communication	05/10/1918	05/10/1918

Heading	War Diary 52nd Divisional Signal Coy From 1st October 1918 To 31st October 1918 Volume XLI With Appendices 1 To 7		
War Diary	Queant	02/10/1918	02/10/1918
War Diary	Cantaing Mill	03/10/1918	06/10/1918
War Diary	Vaulx Vraucourt	07/10/1918	07/10/1918
War Diary	Tincques	08/10/1918	08/10/1918
War Diary	Le Cauroy	09/10/1918	19/10/1918
War Diary	Chateau D'Acq	20/10/1918	20/10/1918
War Diary	Henin Lietard	21/10/1918	22/10/1918
War Diary	Chateau Blanche Maison	24/10/1918	24/10/1918
War Diary	Flines	25/10/1918	29/10/1918
War Diary	Sameon	30/10/1918	31/10/1918
Diagram etc	Diagram		
Heading	War Diary 52nd Lowland Divisional Signal Coy. From 1st November 1918 To 30th November 1918 Volume XLII With Appendices 1 To 5		
War Diary	Sameon	01/11/1918	09/11/1918
War Diary	Mont Du Peruwelz	10/11/1918	10/11/1918
War Diary	Sirault	11/11/1918	16/11/1918
War Diary	Nimy	18/11/1918	30/11/1918
Diagram etc	Diagram		
Heading	War Diary 52nd (Lowland) Divisional Signal Coy. From 1st December 1918 To 31st December 1918 Volume XLIII		
War Diary	Nimy	31/05/1918	31/05/1918
Heading	War Diary 52nd (Lowland) Divisional Signal Coy. From 1st January 1919 To 31st January 1919 Volume XLIV		
War Diary	Nimy	31/01/1919	31/01/1919
Heading	War Diary 52nd (Lowland) Divisional Signal Coy. From 1st Feb 1919 To 28th February 1919 Volume XLV		
War Diary	Nimy	28/02/1919	28/02/1919
Heading	War Diary 52nd (Lowland) Divisional Signal Coy. From 1st March 1919 To 31st March 1919 Volume XLVI		
War Diary	Nimy	01/03/1919	25/03/1919
Heading	War Diary 52nd (Lowland) Divisional Signal Coy From 1st April 1919 To 30th April 1919 Volume XLVII		
War Diary	Soignies	01/04/1919	21/04/1919
Heading	War Diary 52nd Divnl Signal Coy R.E 1st May 1919 To 31st May 1919 Vol XLVIII		
War Diary	Soignies	01/05/1919	27/05/1919

Noes / 2893 (4)

Noes / 2893 (4)

52ND DIVISION

52ND DIVL SIGNAL COY R.E.

APR 1918-MAY 1919

52nd Divisional Engineers

Disembarked MARSEILLES from EGYPT 17.4.18.

52nd DIVISIONAL SIGNAL COMPANY R. E.

APRIL 1918.

WAR DIARY
or
INTELLIGENCE SUMMARY

(Erase heading not required.)

Army Form C. 2118.

Instructions regarding War Diaries and Intelligence Summaries are contained in F.S. Regs., Part II. and the Staff Manual respectively. Title pages will be prepared in manuscript.

Place	Date	Hour	Summary of Events and Information	Remarks and references to Appendices
	1918 April			
JAFFA	1		155 Brigade moved from SARONA to SURAFEND	
LUDD	2	1200	Div HQrs moved to SURAFEND near LUDD. Lieut E. MADGWICK and Lieut A.H. LEEVES joined the Signal Coy.	
	3		156 Brigade entrained at LUDD. 5th (Pioneer) Battn Royal Irish Regt. joined the Division	
	4		157 Brigade moved from SARONA to SURAFEND. All non-technical vehicles & horses handed in.	
	6		157 Brigade entrained at LUDD	
		1200	Signal Office at SURAFEND closed. Handed in all MT vehicles and motor cycles	
		2051	Signal Coy entrained at LUDD	
KANTARA	7	1205	Arrived at KANTARA (EAST)	
	8	0345	Entrained at KANTARA (WEST)	
		1210	Arrived at GABBARY, ALEXANDRIA & embarked on H.M.T.S. INDARRA	
ALEXANDRIA	11	1445	Sailed from ALEXANDRIA. Supplied 4 signallers for duty on bridge of ship.	
MARSEILLES	17	0700	Arrived MARSEILLES and disembarked. Company to rest camp for the night. Major ANGWIN rejoined for duty from leave in England.	

WAR DIARY
INTELLIGENCE SUMMARY

Army Form C. 2118.

Place	Date	Hour	Summary of Events and Information	Remarks and references to Appendices
MARSEILLES	1918 April 18	1327	Entrained at MARSEILLES	
RUE	21	0600	Detrained at NOYELLES-SUR-MER and marched to billets in RUE. Started refitting.	
	24		Lieut H.B. WATERS joined the Coy as Wireless Officer. Diagram of comm'ns is appended	APP. 1
	26		155 Brigade moved to AIRE area	
	28	1530	Closed down signal office at RUE.	
		1744	Entrained at RUE	
AIRE	29	0200	Detrained at AIRE	
	30		Diagram of Communications is appended	APP. 2
			During the month 31 OR joined the Company from E.E.F. Base	
			2 " " " " " B.E.F. "	
			28 OR were attached from R.F.A. to form new artillery subsections	
			11 OR were attached from M.G. and Infantry Battalions to form new No 5 section	
			45 OR were sent to EEF Base as being surplus to French establishment	
			4 OR went to Hospital	

N.G. Alphatski Capt
52 Div. Signal Coy.

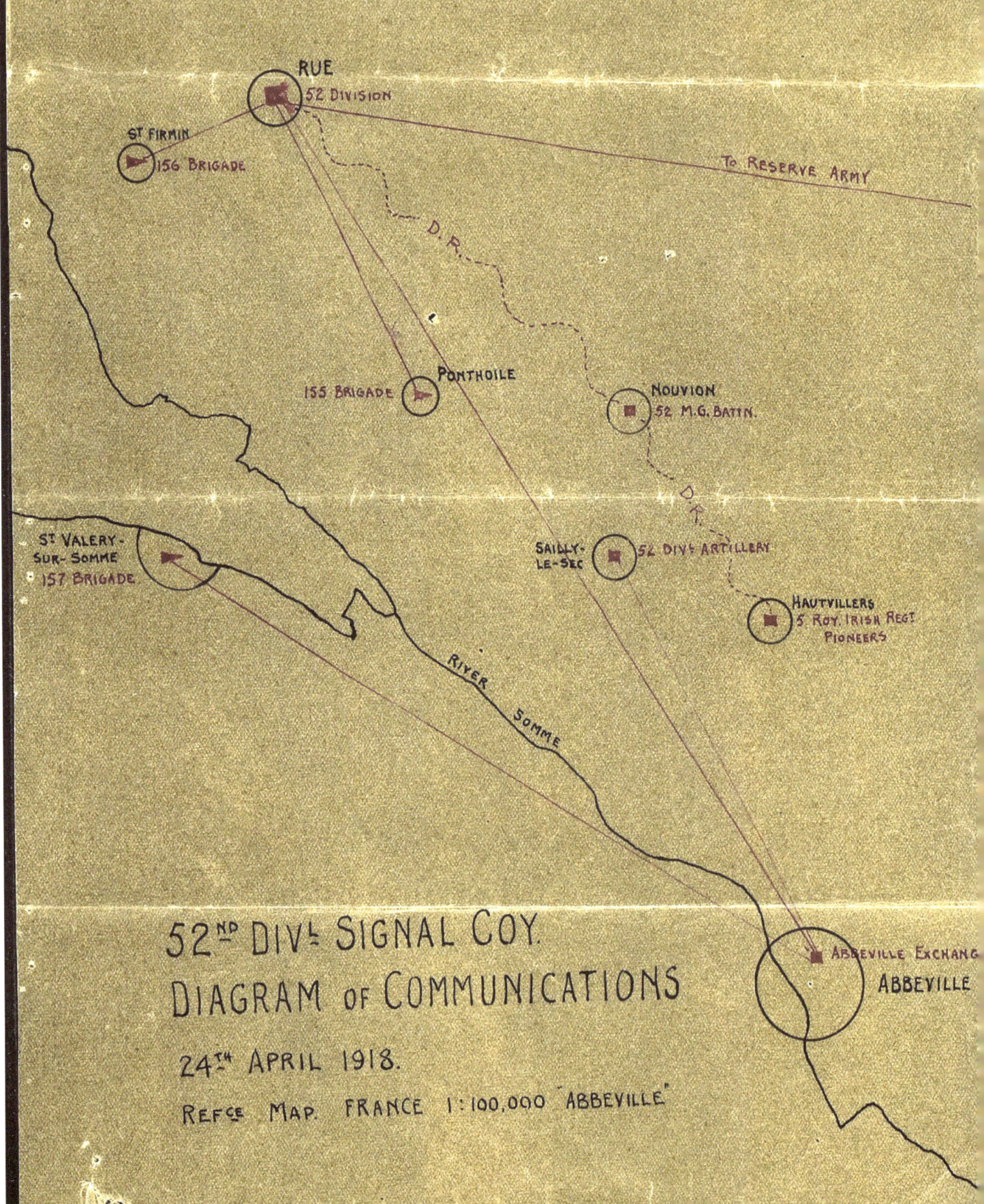

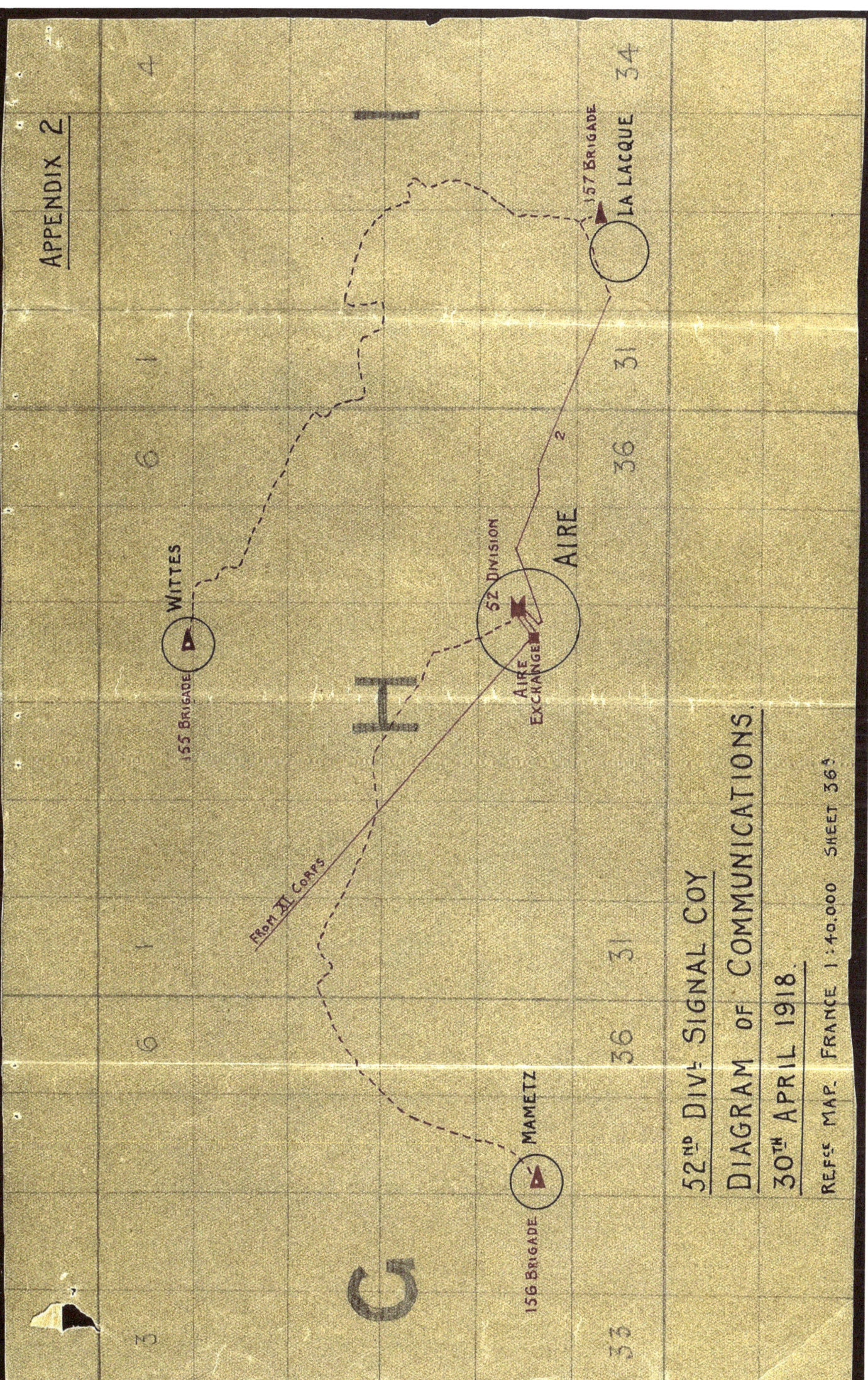

D.a.G.
3rd Echelon
GHQ B.E.F.

Herewith War Diary of this unit Volume XXXV for period 1st/30th April 1918.

Major R.E. (T.)
O.C. Low. Div. Sig. Coy.

4 MAY 1918

ROYAL ENGINEERS.

(Ordinary Trades Only)

Certificate called for by War Office letter No: 30/Engineers/3023 (A.G.7.) dated 15th March 1915.

Certified that No. .... has successfully performed work which in my opinion is equivalent to the test defined in Corps Memo for the (..) rate of Engineer Pay.

Rate to take effect from .... as reported on Army Form B. 213 dated .... 191......

TRADE ....

DATE OF COMPLETION OF TEST ....

Has Present rate been held 6 months ....

Date ....   Officer Commanding

Original

Vol. 2

Confidential.

War Diary.

52nd (Lowland) Divisional Signal Coy R.E.

from 1st May 1918 to 31st May 1918.

VOLUME XXXVI

with Appendix A.

WAR DIARY

Army Form C. 2118.

52ND (LOWLAND) DIVISIONAL SIGNAL COMPANY
No. Vol XXXVI

Place	Date	Hour	Summary of Events and Information	Remarks and references to Appendices
AIRE	1918 MAY 1		Lieut MARSHALL, M.G. Corps, joined the Signal Coy to take charge of the newly formed No.5 section.	
	4		The R.A. Hqrs detachment and the two R.F.A. signal subsections joined their respective Hqrs.	
	6	1700	A signal office was opened at Chateau d'Acq	
		1908	The Coy entrained at AIRE and proceeded to ACQ. The signal office at AIRE was left open as all the Brigades had not moved to the new area.	
		0600	157 Brigade moved from LELACQUE to NEUVILLE ST VAAST	
			52 Div. Artillery Brigade took over from 5th Canadian Div. Artillery Brigade at AUX RIETZ	
CHATEAU D'ACQ	7	0700	Brigade's took over from 4 Canadian Div'l Brigade	
		1000	Div'l Artillery Hqrs moved from AUX RIETZ to CHATEAU D'ACQ	
			157 Brigade moved from NEUVILLE ST VAAST and went into the line in the left section of the div'l sector.	

WAR DIARY
or
INTELLIGENCE SUMMARY.
(Erase heading not required.)

Army Form C. 2118.

Place	Date	Hour	Summary of Events and Information	Remarks and references to Appendices
CHATEAU D'ACQ	1918 MAY 8		156 Bde moved to NEUVILLE ST VAAST	
	9		155 Bde went into the line in the right section of the Div'l sector. 156 Bde moved to MONT ST ELOY (Reserve Bde position) The old & Canad. Div'l Hqrs Signal Office at AUX RIETZ was made into an advanced Div'l Hqrs Signal Office. It transmitted messages to the Brigades. Owing to shortage of lines between CHATEAU D'ACQ and AUX RIETZ 'Phone calls between A.H.Q. & Bdes were put thro' AUX RIETZ exchange & a regular DRLS A DR.L.S. started. 3 runs per day to each Brigade.	
	11		Two new lines between Div & AUX RIETZ having been obtained, it was possible to put the two Bdes on the line thro' to the Div without switching at AUX RIETZ.	
	13	0900	The Div'l Artillery circuits were taken out of the Signal Office & put into a separate Art. Signal Office. 2/Lt J.G.T. Hiley was attached to the Coy as a supernumerary Officer.	
	15		156 Bde relieved 155 Bde in the right section.	

WAR DIARY
or
INTELLIGENCE SUMMARY

Army Form C. 2118.

Place	Date	Hour	Summary of Events and Information	Remarks and references to Appendices
CHATEAU D'ACQ	1918 MAY 16		Lieut H.D. HANBURY To hospital sick.	
	24		155 Brigade relieved 157 Brigade in the left section. 157 Bde went into reserve.	
	27		Div¹ H.Qrs was shelled by H.V. gun. It was decided to construct an emergency signal office 500 yds away. A diagram of communications as at this date is appended	Appendix "A"
	29		The emergency signal office was completed. + cables laid and buried connecting it with the main signal office, and the main aerial route going round and the main signal office.	
			Practice in aeroplane contact work was carried out by battalions of the 157 Bde (in reserve)	
	30		A demonstration of the use of message carrying rockets was carried out at the 157 Bde Hqrs MONT ST ELOY.	

Army Form C. 2118.

WAR DIARY
or
INTELLIGENCE SUMMARY.
(Erase heading not required.)

Place	Date	Hour	Summary of Events and Information	Remarks and references to Appendices
CHATEAU D'ACQ	1918 MAY		During the month short courses for Battalion signalling Officers and signallers were held at Div Hqrs. There were attended by personnel from the Bde in reserve. These courses directed attention to the differences between intercommunication in France and in Palestine.	
			Brigade pools of battalion signallers were formed and courses of instruction in Power Buzzer, Amplifier and Trench mirror were held at Div Hqrs. Some of the pd men were sent to the 1st Army Wireless School. Five men of the Signal Coy wireless section were sent on a six weeks course at the 1st Army Wireless School.	
			A regular supply of pigeons (4 per Brigade) was sent to Bdes in the line, both Infantry and Artillery. All pigeons were released with messages from posts in the line successfully	

WAR DIARY
or
INTELLIGENCE SUMMARY

(Erase heading not required.)

Army Form C. 2118.

[Stamp: 52ND (LOWLAND) DIVISIONAL SIGNAL COMPANY]

Place	Date	Hour	Summary of Events and Information	Remarks and references to Appendices
CHATEAU D'ACQ	1916 MAY		About 4 courses of instruction for pigeoneers were held at the Coy. allotted to the Div. 50 men passed there courses successfully. During the month 19 OR's went to hospital sick and 1 OR wounded 25 OR's joined from the Base as reinforcements.	

N.G. Gilpatrick Capt.
52 Divl. Signal Coy.

52ND DIVL SIGNAL COY.

DIAGRAM OF COMMUNICATIONS

27TH MAY 1918.

REF. MAP "MAROEUIL" 1:20,000.

NOTE.
ARTILLERY COMMNS IN RED
INFANTRY " BLUE
AERIAL ROUTES ....
GROUND CABLE ....
BURIED CABLE ....
W/T COMMNS ....
P.B.A

Appendix "A"

Confidential.

War Diary.

52nd Divisional Signal Coy. R.E.

From 1st June 1918 to 30th June 1918.

Volume XXXVII

Army Form C. 2118.

WAR DIARY
or
INTELLIGENCE SUMMARY
(*Erase heading not required.*)

Place	Date	Hour	Summary of Events and Information	Remarks and references to Appendices
FRANCE. MAROEUIL SHEET - A.3.b.5.2.	1/6/18		Battn billeted in Cellar Camp, Neuville St Vast. (Less A Coy at Villers aux Bois) A Coy working on improvement in trenches.	G.S.G
			Working on Shelters, Pipe Line, & Hutting of Div H.Q.	
	2nd June		D Coy provided ATCs in charge in Wilbershal Ssector of Trenches. Relieved by	
	9th June		C Coy & working on front line repair. Returned to Cellar Camp 12th June.	G.S.G
	10th June		A Coy concentrated at Battn H.Q.	
	11th June		Outbreak of P.U.O. (Trench fever): spread rapidly over 30 men sick at one time: total eventually sick = 514 in all.	G.S.G
	30th June		Orders to convert Battn from a Battn of Railway Troops to a Pioneer Battn: & posted to 52nd Division received.	G.S.G
			Casualties. 1. O.R. died of wounds. 2 O.R died of sickness	
			7. O.R. wounded	
			3. O.R. " slightly (at duty)	G.S.G

Ses Unwin
Capt & Adjutant.
For O.C. 17th North'd Fus.

2449 Wt. W14957/M90 750,000 1/16 J.B.C. & A. Forms/C.2118/12.

WAR DIARY
INTELLIGENCE SUMMARY

(Erase heading not required.)

Place	Date	Hour	Summary of Events and Information	Remarks and references to Appendices
CHATEAU D'ACQ	1918 June 8		From 8.0 am 8th till 8.0 am 9th was a "silent" period. No 'phone conversations were allowed.	
	13		A Divisional Signal School was started for 30 NCo's and men from each of the three brigades. Each course is to last 6 weeks.	
	15		An old German bury from TM test point (T30C41) to T21 Central in the D.I. sector was tested through and made available for use.	
	17		An aeroplane contact practice was carried out by the 155 Bde. (in reserve) with good results.	
	20	12.55 am	An aeroplane bomb fell in the road opposite the M.G. Battn Hqrs. The signal office was wrecked. 2 men were killed. 6 were wounded all of No 5 Section of the Coy.	
	22		A new bury from SV test point (S23 C 64) to SL test point (S24 A 20) was finished.	
	26		A new bury from TR test point (T26 C 54) to BF test point (B8 D 95) was begun. This is to serve 3 new battalion hqrs along railway embankment.	
	28		Lt A.M. Nisbet was detailed to attend a 3 weeks W/T course at 1st Army School.	

WAR DIARY
INTELLIGENCE SUMMARY.

Place	Date	Hour	Summary of Events and Information	Remarks and references to Appendices
CHATEAU D'ACQ	1918 June		During the month, in addition to casualties reported 20th. 11 OR went to hospital sick 7 OR returned from hospital 6 OR joined the Coy from the base	N.G. Copestake Capt. 52 Div Sig Coy.

Vol 4

Confidential

War Diary

52nd Divnl Signal Coy.

From. 1st July 1918 to 31st July 1918.

VOLUME XXXVIII

with Appendices 1 and 2.

Army Form C. 2118.

WAR DIARY
or
INTELLIGENCE SUMMARY.
(Erase heading not required.)

Instructions regarding War Diaries and Intelligence Summaries are contained in F. S. Regs., Part II. and the Staff Manual respectively. Title pages will be prepared in manuscript.

Place	Date	Hour	Summary of Events and Information	Remarks and references to Appendices
CHATEAU D'ACQ	1918 July 2		The new 20-pair bury behind LENS-ARRAS Railway between Mersey Alley and Tired Alley was finished.	
	20		157 Brigade moved from Reserve position to AUCHEL, where communication to them was obtained through 13th Corps at FERFAY	
	21		156 Brigade was relieved in the right sector by 233rd Brigade of the 8th Div. 156 Brigade moved to Reserve position MONT ST ELOI	
	22		156 Brigade moved to BARLIN, where their communication was thro' 1st Army ad. office BARLIN.	
			155 Brigade was relieved in the left sector by 24th Brigade and moved to VERDREL, where its communication was by telephone to CUPIGNY Exchange. Diagram of circulation is appended	APP 1
	23	12 noon	Divl Signal Office closed at CHATEAU D'ACQ and opened at PERNES The Divl Signal School closed and instructors & pupils returned to their units. The Div. was relieved by the 5th Div. & went into 17th Corps Diagram of communications is appended	APP 2

WAR DIARY
or
INTELLIGENCE SUMMARY.
(Erase heading not required.)

Army Form C. 2118.

Place	Date	Hour	Summary of Events and Information	Remarks and references to Appendices
PERNES	1918 July 30		156 Bde moved from BARLIN to ECOIVRES, where communication to them was obtained through 4th Canadian Div.	
			157 Bde moved from AUCHEL to BARLIN, where they took over from the 156 Bde.	
			An advance party was sent from Div. Hqrs to MAROEUIL preparatory to taking over from 4th Canadian Div.	
	31		156 Bde went into the right section of the Div. sector	
			155 Bde moved from VERDREL to ROCLINCOURT & took over the left section	
			157 Bde moved from BARLIN to MADAGASCAR CAMP.	
			While the Div. Hqrs were at PERNES a regular DRLS was maintained direct with all Brigades and Div. Artillery Hqrs at CUVIGNY	
			Casualties, etc during the month	
			5/7/18 Lt. Hanbury rejoined from hospital	
			17/7/18 Lt. J.G.T. Miles left to rejoin 1st Army Signal Coy	
			Lt. A.V. Johnson attached from the Base.	

Army Form C. 2118.

WAR DIARY
or
~~INTELLIGENCE~~ SUMMARY
(Erase heading not required.)

Instructions regarding War Diaries and Intelligence Summaries are contained in F. S. Regs., Part II. and the Staff Manual respectively. Title pages will be prepared in manuscript.

Place	Date	Hour	Summary of Events and Information	Remarks and references to Appendices
	1918 July			
	21/7/18		Lieut Marshall was taken on strength of Company	
			During the month	
			12 other ranks were sent to hospital sick	
			2 do do wounded	
			5 do rejoined from hospital	
			12 do joined as reinforcements from Base.	

J.G. Capstick Capt.
~~Major R.E. (T)~~
for O.C. Low. Div. Sig. Coy.

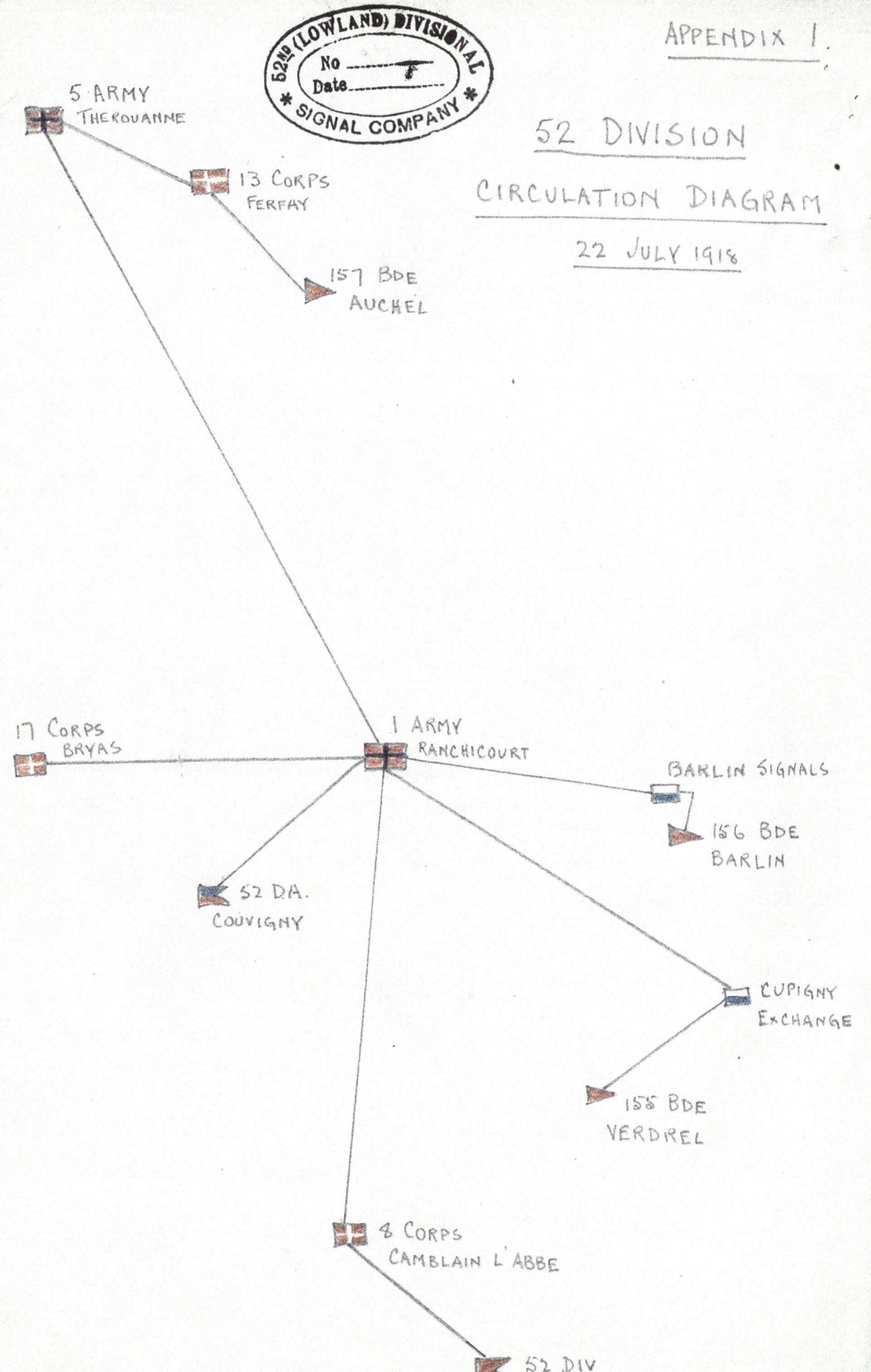

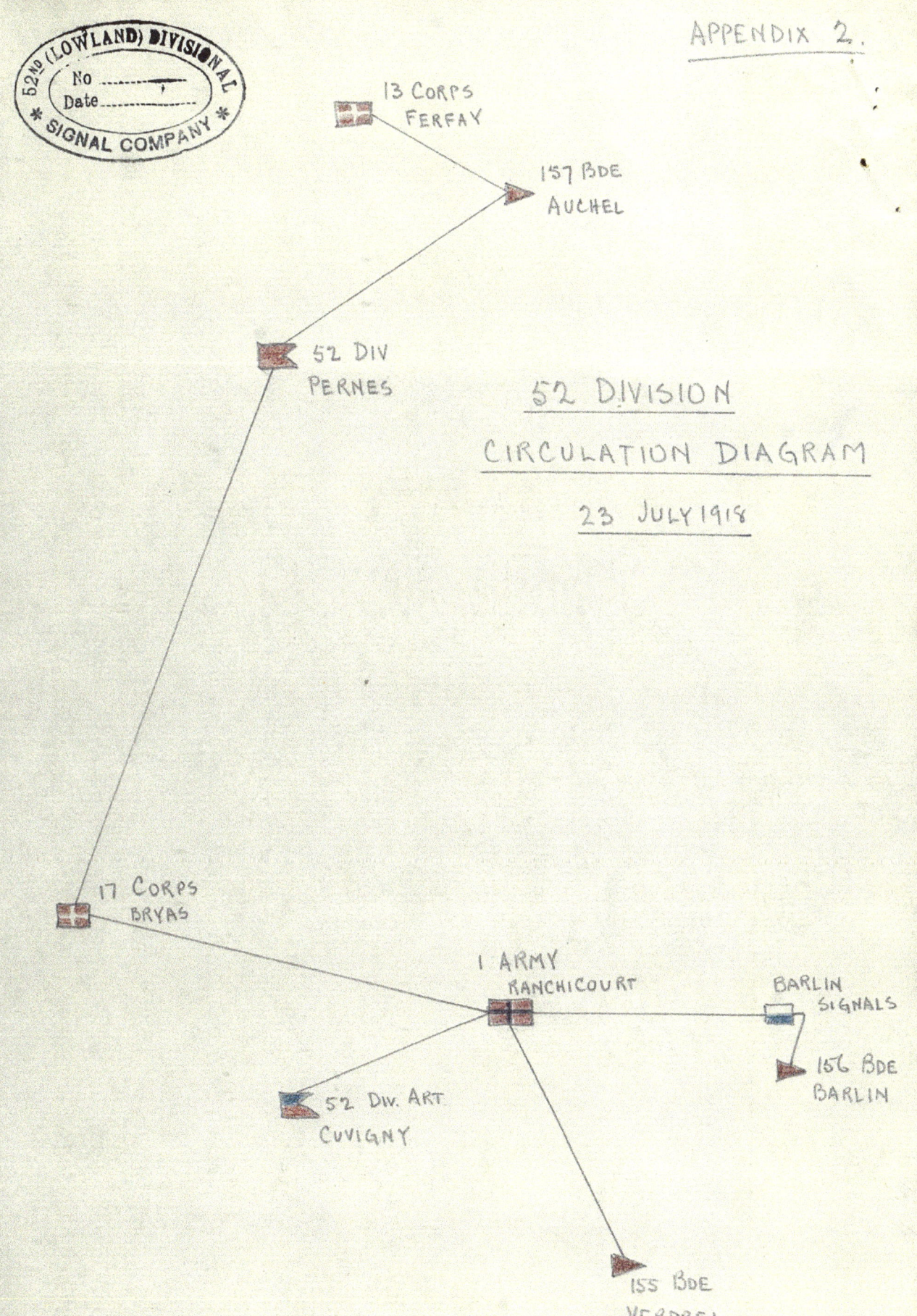

WAR DIARY or INTELLIGENCE SUMMARY

Army Form C. 2118.

52D Signals Vol 5

Place	Date	Hour	Summary of Events and Information	Remarks and references to Appendices
PERNES	1914 Aug. 2		The Division relieved 4th Canadian Division in the line WILLERVAL, GAVRELLE. Div. Hq. moved to MAREOEUIL. All existing communications were taken over. 155 Bde in the line on left, 152 Bde on right, 157 Bde in centre. All Bdes were on the buried system. An advanced comm- centre was opened just west of ECURIE. The usual system of comm by wireless, Power Buzzer, Amplifier, pigeons & message carrying rockets were arranged. Visual comm. was most difficult owing to the nature of the ground. Two of the Bde Hqrs were on the front slope of the ridge.	
MAROEUIL	14/16		The Division was relieved partly by 8th Div- partly by 51st Div. Communications were handed over as they stood with slight modifications.	
	16	0900	Div Hqrs moved to VILLERS CHATEL, where communications were taken over from 51st Division. Diagram is appended.	APP. 1
VILLERS CHATEL	20	.	155 Bde moved to HAMBARQ, 152 Bde to BERNEVILLE, 157 Bde to AGNEZ-LES-DUISANS. An advance Div. Office was opened at HERMAVILLE.	
	21	0800	Div. Hqrs moved to HERMAVILLE. Diagram of communications is appended	APP 2

Army Form C. 2118.

WAR DIARY
or
~~INTELLIGENCE SUMMARY.~~
(Erase heading not required.)

Instructions regarding War Diaries and Intelligence Summaries are contained in F. S. Regs., Part II. and the Staff Manual respectively. Title pages will be prepared in manuscript.

Place	Date 1916 Aug.	Hour	Summary of Events and Information	Remarks and references to Appendices
HERMAVILLE	22	1300	Div. Hqrs moved to BRETEN COURT. 155 Bde moved to BARLY, 156 Bde to BLAIREVILLE, 157 Bde to BRETENCOURT. The divl Office at HERMAVILLE was kept open until all the Bdes had moved down to Bdes in their new positions was this the existing lines of the communn to Bdes in their new positions was thro' the existing lines of the 59th Div. The 155 Bde at BARLY were connected to BAVINCOURT exchange.	
BRETENCOURT	23		156 Bde attacked. After dark, 3 pairs of twisted cable were laid from the most advanced point of the buried system to a point about one mile eastward. These were laid in a continuous chain by the pioneer battalion.	
	24	0800	Div. Hqrs moved to BLAIREVILLE QUARRY. 156 and 157 Bdes attacked. ~~The Div. was~~ All Bde Hqrs moved forward. Cable wagons moved forward with Bdes and kept them in touch by wire. Bdes were also accompanied by wireless stations. An advanced communication centre was established at the head of the buried cable.	
BLAIREVILLE QUARRY	24/28		Notes on signal communications during the operations are appended.	APP. 3
	25		Diagram of communications at Div Hqrs which got in touch with Bdes and M.G. Corps. The divl wireless station were near the adv. commn centre.	APP. 4

Army Form C. 2118.

WAR DIARY
or
INTELLIGENCE SUMMARY.
(Erase heading not required.)

Instructions regarding War Diaries and Intelligence Summaries are contained in F. S. Regs., Part II. and the Staff Manual respectively. Title pages will be prepared in manuscript.

Place	Date 1918	Hour	Summary of Events and Information	Remarks and references to Appendices
BLAIREVILLE QUARRY	Aug 27-28	0800	Diagram of communications is appended. The 31st Div was relieved by the 57th Div. who opened Hqrs at head of buried cable & took over lines forward. 52 Div Bdes came back to positions near head of buried cable for 3 days rest.	APP. 5
	30		Diagram of communications to Bdes is appended	APP. 6
	31		An advance Office was opened at cross roads west of CROISILLES. All Bde Hqrs moved to area north of CROISILLES.	
	31	1600	Div. Hqrs moved to CROISILLES. Casualties and reinforcements:- On 30th Lieut C.E. WEEDS went to hospital sick During the month 10 O.R. went to hospital sick 2 do do wounded 2 O.R. were killed 6 O.R. rejoined from hospital 10 O.R. reinforcements were received.	

M.G. Postath Capt.
52 Div. Signal Coy

APPENDIX 1.

157 Bde.
Chateau
de la Haie.

155 Bde.
Caucourt.

M.G. Battⁿˢ
Cambligneul.

52 DIV
Villers Chatel.

R.A.
Aubigny.

8ᵗʰ Corps.
Camblain
l'Abbe.

17ᵗʰ Corps.
Duisans.

156 Bde.
Chateau
Berles.

52 SIGNALS
17/8/18.

REF. MAP "LEN 11" 1/100,000

APPENDIX 2.

I Corps
Duisans

157 Bde
Agnen les Duisans

155 Bde
Habareq

156 Bde
Berneville

Villers Chatel

R.A. Aubigny

52 DIV.
Hermaville

21/8/18.   REF. MAP. "LENS 11" 1/100,000

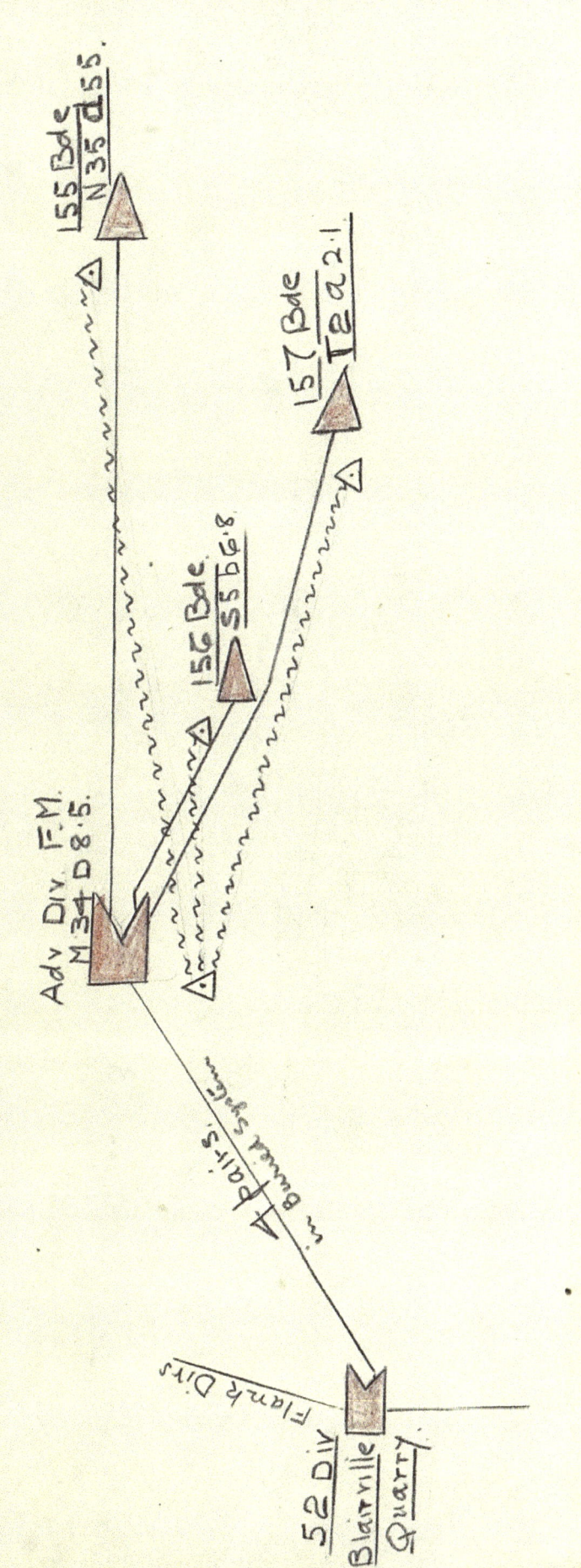

APPENDIX 5.

156 Bde
N34a6·6

156 Bde
T5a8·4

157 Bde
T10b6·2

Advd Comn Centre
F.M. M34d5·8

52 DIV.
Blairville Quarry.

4 pairs

Flank Divs

27/8/18.

SHEET 51B. 1/40,000

APPENDIX 6.

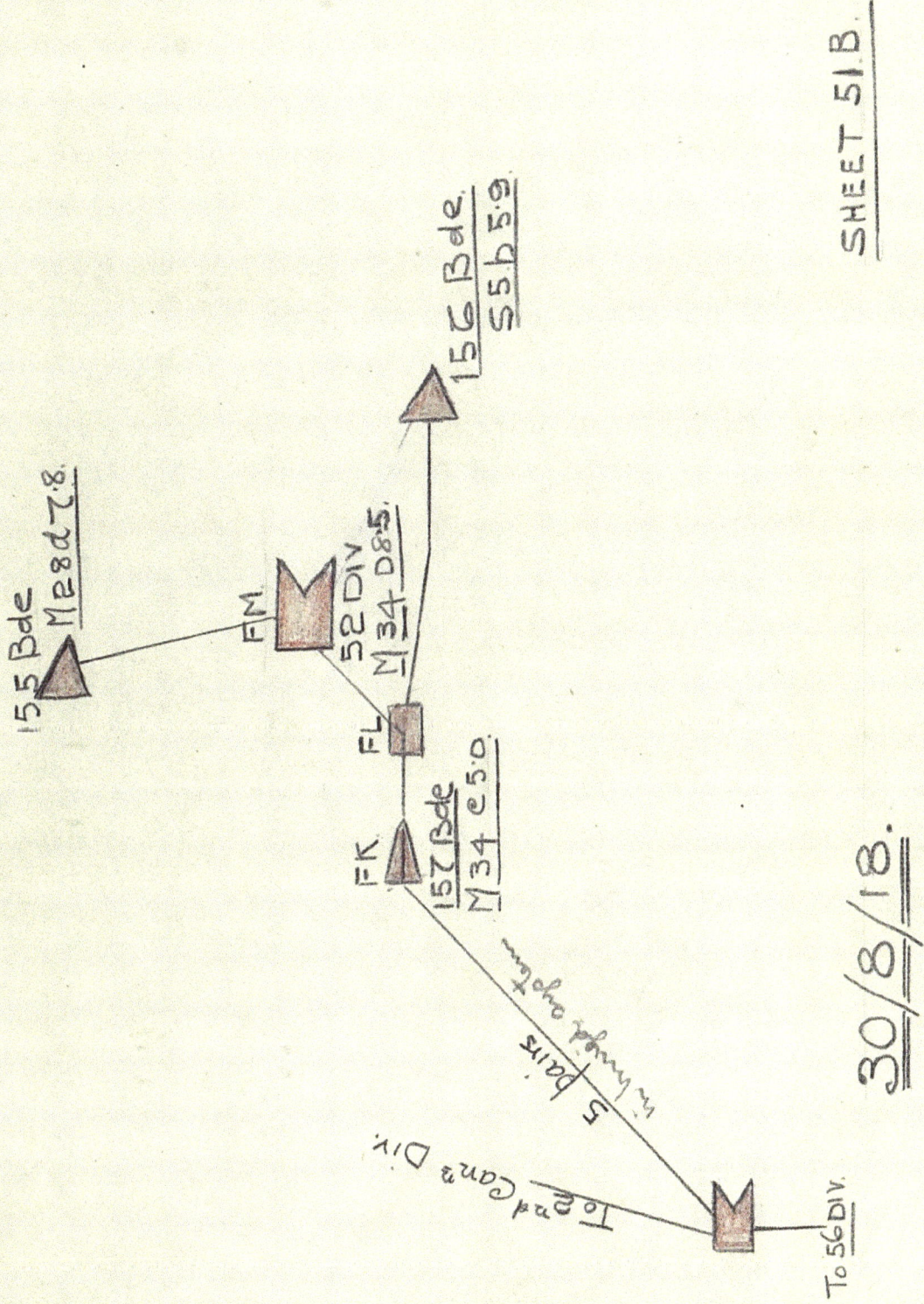

SHEET 51.B. 1/40000

30/8/18.

Signal Communications during Operations 23rd to 24th August.

I. Division to Brigades.

(a) Telegraph and Telephone. Divisional Headquarters were situated at a test point on the buried system. Lines to Brigades were provided on the buried system to a test box 3 miles forward where the system terminates. From there to Brigades field cable was used. An advanced Communication Centre was established at the end of the buried system. The buried cables were not in good order, there was a loss of insulation which resulted in poor speaking when the lines were extended forward. The loss was not sufficient to interfere with telegraph work. Intermediate test stations were established between advanced communication centre and the Brigades. Interruptions on the field cables were few and quickly made good.

(b) Wireless.

French wireless sets were allotted to each brigade and the Divisional Station erected at the forward communication centre.

The set with "A" Brigade worked satisfactorily throughout and was moved forward with each move of the Brigade. Difficulty was experienced with the set with "C" Brigade owing to its getting out of adjustment in transit. This set was carried by hand for a considerable distance. "B" Brigade did not carry forward its wireless when moving to advanced headquarters and it was not of much service at the position it was left.

No pack animals were provided for the transport forward of wireless sets and it is necessary to utilise one of the Brigade section horses. If a horse cannot be taken forward three additional men from the Brigade are necessary to carry the set.

(C) Visual.

A central visual station was established but little use was made of it. Distances were too great for Lucas lamps by day and helio was uncertain. The provision of additional transmitting stations was not considered desirable in view of the personnel required and that other alternatives were available.

(D). Dispatch Riders.

Mounted orderlies and motor cyclists were used, the former were employed principally as guides and to carry forward pigeons. Motor Cyclist DRs were able to get nearly up to Brigade Headquarters and dealt with all the dispatch work.

II Forward of Brigades.

Field cable, Visual, pigeons and runners were all used to varying extents. 'B' Brigade relied entirely on field cable and runners, and did not use visual owing to the unfavourable positions of headquarters of units. In 'C' Brigade visual communications were so satisfactory that the bulk of the message work was done by lamps and lines used chiefly for telephone conversations and priority messages. Excellent results were obtained from pigeons in this Brigade. 'A' Brigade used their pigeons for supply and transport messages 'B' Brigade made little use of them. Fullerphones were not used. All telegraph work was done on D III instrument.

III. Artillery.

The communications to six Brigades of Artillery arranged in two groups were found to be difficult with the frequent movements. The additional lines required from groups to sub-groups had to be laid by the telephone wagon of the Brigade sub-section in addition to its normal work of connecting up batteries. Heavy demands for cable, result as there is not time for the recovery of lines when the forward move takes place. Two heavy Brigades were attached to the Division, no cable wagon is provided to maintain communication to them from Division. Difficulty was experienced in maintaining communication when the moves of the Heavy Brigades occurred at the same time as the advance of the Infantry Brigades. C.W. sets would have proved of great value during these operations for artillery communications.

IV. Office Work.

The number of messages dealt with was considerable. 874 telegrams were dealt with at Divisional Headquarters Signal Office on one day and 180 packets sent by D.R.L.S. and special messenger. Included in this total are 81 "Urgent Operation" and 33 "Priority" messages. As only single circuits could be provided to Brigades during the frequent moves, the disposal of this large volume of traffic was difficult when the lines were frequently engaged by telephone conversation. Illegibility of carbon copies of multiple address messages is a source of delay in transmission.

It was not generally understood that after Zero hour training manual signalling calls should be used instead of code calls. A very large percentage of telephone calls were passed as "Urgent Operation."

V. Casualties were high in battalion signal personnel. As a result some units were unable to recover articles of signalling equipment which were taken into action.

VI. Contact Aeroplane reception and transmission of messages by this means appeared to work very satisfactorily.

VII. Power Buzzers & Amplifiers. These were not used after the first advance. They were held in reserve ready to be sent forward if required.

Confidential

War Diary
52nd Lowland Divisional Signal Coy
from 1/9/15 to 30/9/15

Volume XL
with appendices 1-6

WAR DIARY or INTELLIGENCE SUMMARY

Army Form C. 2118.

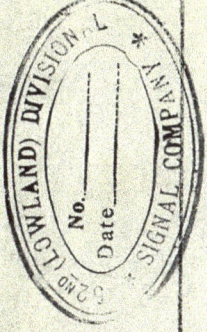
52nd (LOWLAND) DIVISIONAL SIGNAL COMPANY

Place	Date 1918	Hour	Summary of Events and Information	Remarks
CROISILLES	Sept. 1		A troop of yeomanry was attached to Signals for duty as mounted D.Rs. Three were sent to each infantry Bde.	
	2		Lieut C.E. Weeds went to hospital sick.	
	4		Lieut LAWSON joined for duty, as supernumerary officer.	
	5		An advanced communication centre was established in HINDENBURG LINE SW of QUEANT. Diagram of communications is appended	APP. 1
	6		During the afternoon and evening night all Inf. Bdes moved into reserve in the ST LEGER area. Lines were laid direct to them from Div Hq.	
	15	1600	155 Bde moved to DIUS, who took over the existing communications to the front	
			Handed over to 57 Div, who took over the existing communications to the front	
	17	1000	Div Hq moved to QUEANT and took over from 57 Div. The Div Hq was established at 57 Div near Hqrs and a test point at 57 advanced Hqrs. This made it unnecessary to rearrange the existing lines, but no fresh cable was laid except for artillery.	
QUEANT		2400	An enemy aeroplane bomb fell in the Coy horse lines and killed 14 horses and wounded 8. The plane was afterwards brought down in flames. Lieut Capt McMichael to hospital wounded at 157 Bde Hqrs.	
	19	1900	155 Bde attacked and retook MOEUVRES. During the night 157 Bde was relieved in the left section of the divisional front by	

Army Form C. 2118.

WAR DIARY
or
INTELLIGENCE SUMMARY.
(Erase heading not required.)

Instructions regarding War Diaries and Intelligence Summaries are contained in F. S. Regs., Part II. and the Staff Manual respectively. Title pages will be prepared in manuscript.

Place	Date 1918	Hour	Summary of Events and Information	Remarks and references to Appendices
QUEANT	Sept 19		A Brigade of the 2 Canadian Div.	
			A Div. Signalling School was formed at 2 Div. Reception Camp. The instructional staff was drawn from the Infantry of the division. 112 students started.	
	20		157 Bde withdrew to a reserve position near NOREUIL	
			Diagram of communications is appended	APP 2
			Lieut FETHERSTON HAUGH was attached as supernumerary Officer.	
	24		Lieut FETHERSTON HAUGH left to take up another appointment. Lieut LAZARUS joined for duty as supernumerary Officer.	
	26	1800	An advanced Div. Hqrs. Dz&B17 about 570. Div. Hqrs at QUEANT.	
	27	0520	Div. took part in an attack.	
			A diagram of communications as at ZERO hour for Infantry is appended	APP 3
			Also "Appendix D to Div. Order No. 136. "Communications."	APP 4
			Also a diagram of artillery communications	APP 5
	28th 30th		Bns in reserve	

Army Form C. 2118.

WAR DIARY
or
INTELLIGENCE SUMMARY.
(Erase heading not required.)

Place	Date	Hour	Summary of Events and Information	Remarks and references to Appendices
			Casualties during September.	
			KILLED 3 other Ranks	
			WOUNDED 10 "	
			SICK 14 "	
			REINFORCEMENTS 5 "	
			REJOINED FROM HOSPITAL 4 "	
			An appendix on Commendation during operations is attached	Append. 6
			During the month the following decorations were awarded	
			415043 Sgt. Mackae A awarded Military Medal	
			418077 " Weston J " D.C.M.	
			418024 Spr. Perry H.E. " Military Medal	
			501187 " Ford J.S " Military Medal	
			10 OCT 1918	

Signed: Major R.E.(T.)
O.C. Low. Div. Sig. Coy

APPENDIX I

155 C6a5.9
156 D1a3.2
Adv. D1C6.0
157 D7a1.9
Single D5
Air line Head U24
5¹ DIV
T4b
U27c
BULLECOURT.
TEST
TP2a
CROISSELLES.
GUARDS DIV.
B17 a 88.

All D8 twin except where marked.

REF. MAP. SHEETS 51B.57C.

52 DIV. 5-9-1918.

[Stamp: 52ND (LOWLAND) DIVISIONAL SIGNAL COMPANY]

[Signature] Major R.E. (¹)
O.C. Low. Div. Sig. Coy.

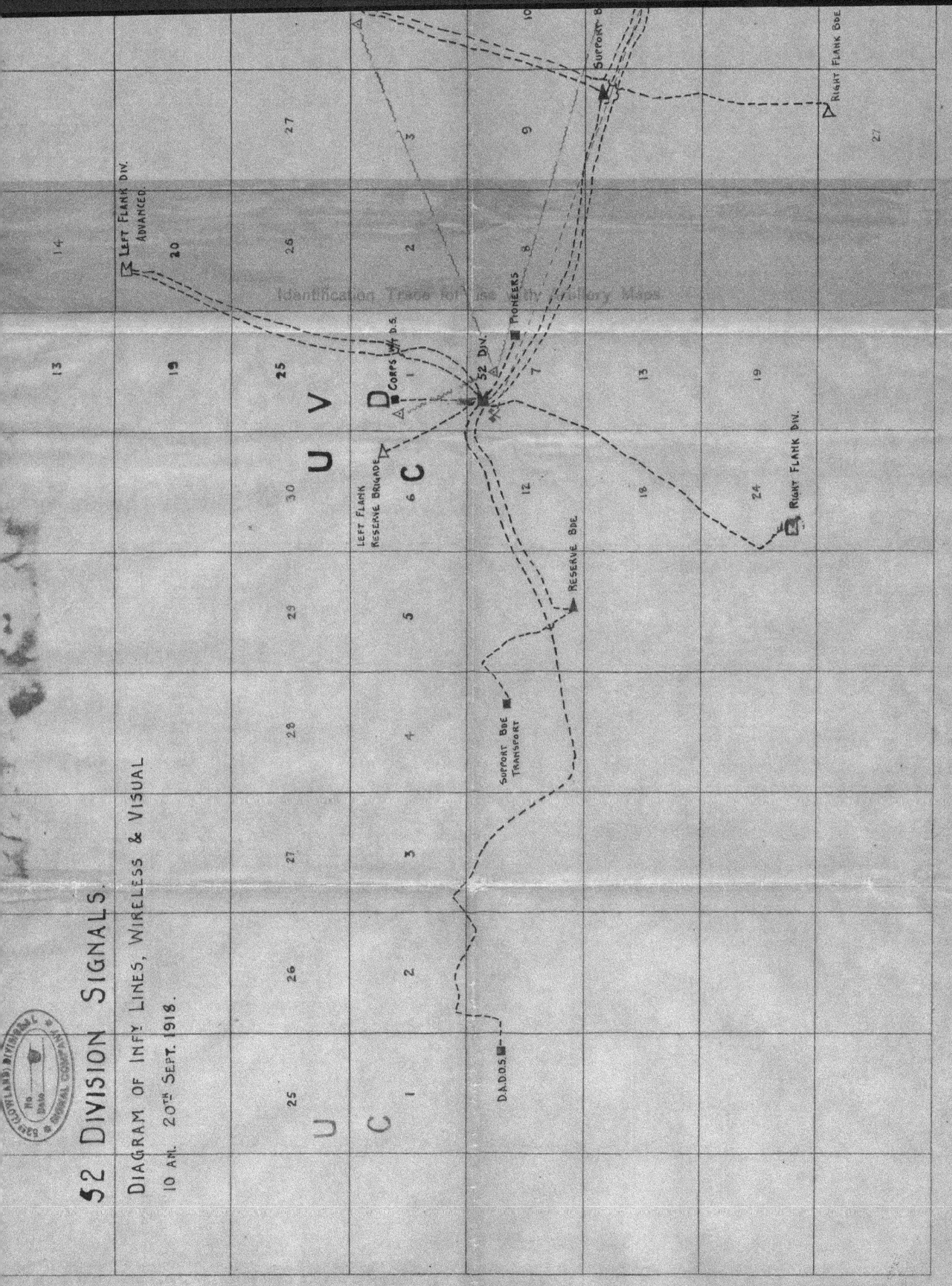

Identification Trace for use with Artillery Maps.

APPENDIX 2.

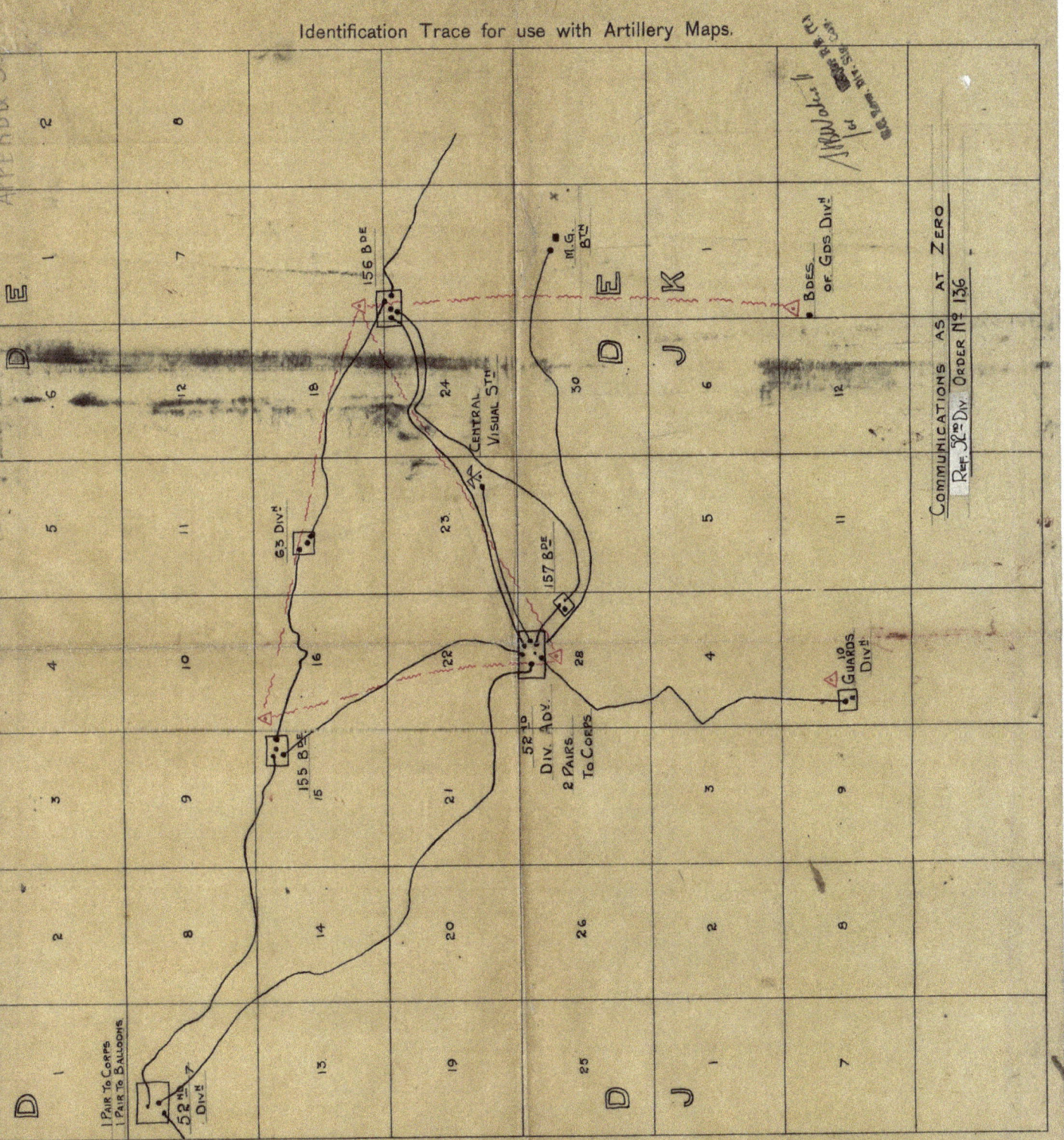

SECRET.   Copy No. 15

APPENDIX 'D'
TO
52nd DIVISION ORDER No. 136.

25th September, 1918.

COMMUNICATIONS.

TELEGRAPH & TELEPHONE.   1.   The main cable lines provided for the initial stage are shown on the accompanying diagram (issued to those marked #).

These cables will be extended to Brigades as they move forward.

All units have their establishment of Cable in possession.

WIRELESS.   2.   The Corps Directing Station is at Sheet 51.C. C.9.b.4.4.

At Zero hour the Divisional Station will be moved from its present position to D.28.b.1.7.

Each Brigade will erect its Trench Wireless Set at Battle Hd.Qrs. ready to open at Zero Hour. One pair of loop sets will be issued to 156th and 157th Brigades.

P.B.A's will be held at Advanced Divisional Headquarters for issue as required, when positions have been consolidated.

Small charging set will be at Advanced Divisional Hd.Qrs.

VISUAL.   3.   A Central Visual Station will be established at D.23.d.8.5. and connected by 'phone to Advanced Divisional Hd.Qrs.

This station will be manned by No. 5 Section, Divisional Signal Company, and is available for communication to all units.   Station Call = YEBR.

PIGEONS.   4.   Pigeons will be distributed to Brigades and Artillery according to the number available, which will probably be from 24 to 30.

CONTACT AEROPLANE.   5.   The Divisional Dropping Station will be at D.28.b.1.7.

Ground Sheets will be displayed at all Brigade and Battalion Hd.Qrs.

DISPATCH RIDER.   6.   Motor-cyclist D.Rs. have been distributed
     1 to each Inf. Brigade.
     2 to Artillery.
     4 at Corps Hd.Qrs.
     8 at Divisional Hd.Qrs.
Mounted Dispatch Riders are not available.

Lieut-Colonel,
General Staff,
52nd Division.

Issued at ... 7 pm

P.T.O.

```
Copy No. 1 to  G.O.C.
         2     'G'.
       3-4     'A' & 'Q'.
         5     155th Inf. Bde.      *
         6     156th Inf. Bde.      *
         7     157th Inf. Bde.      *
         8     C.R.A.
         9     C.R.E.
        10     M.G. Battn.          *
        11     17th N.F. (P).
        12     A.D.M.S.
        13     D.A.D.V.S.
        14     Div. Train.
        15     Div. Signal Coy.     *
        16     D.A.P.M.
        17     Div. M.T. Coy.
        18     D.A.D.O.S.
        19     S.G.O.
        20     Camp Commandant.
     21-22     XVII Corps.          *
        23     XVII Corps H.A.
        24     63rd Division.       *
     25-26     Guards Division.     *
     27-28     2nd Canadian Division.
        29     13th Squadn. R.A.F.  *
     30-31     Diary.
        32     'B' Coy. 15th Bn., Tank Corps.
        33     43rd Balloon Section.
        34     4th Canadian Division.
        35     57th Division.
```

Identification Trace for use with Artillery Maps.

APPENDIX 5

D					D	E	
1	2	3	4	5	6	1	2
7	8	9	10	11	12	7	8
13	14	15	56 B de 16	63 R.A. 17	18	13	14
19	20	21	22	23	24	19	20
			52 D.A.				
25	26	27	28	29	30	25	26
D					D	E	
J					J	K	
1	2	3	4	5	6	1	2
7	8	9	9th Bde 10	72 Bde 11	93 Bde 12	7	8
13	14	15	16	17	18	13	14

NOTE.—(1). These traces are intended to facilitate the communication of information as to the position of targets, which have been located on a squared map.
(2). The squares on this trace are 500 yards in length on the 1/10,000 scale, 1,000 yards in length on the 1/20,000 scale, and 2,000 yards in length on the 1/40,000 scale.
(3). The squares on the trace are fitted to the squares of the map showing the targets, which are then drawn on the trace. Sufficient letters and numbers must also be added to enable the recipient to place the trace in the correct position on his own map. A little detail may also be traced, but this is not essential. The name and scale of the map to which the trace refers must be always given. The trace can be used for the 1/10,000, 1/20,000 or 1/40,000 scale.

G.S.G.S. 3025.

DIAGRAM OF COMMUNICATIONS
52 DIV ARTILLERY
AT ZERO.

Tracing taken from Sheet 57c NE.

of the 1:20,000 map of FRANCE

Signature .... Date ....

M G Wakeell
for
O.C. Low Div. Sig. Coy
Major R.E. (T.)

Appendix 6

Report on Communications during recent Operations

Field Cable

Twisted cable was used to the Headquarters of formations in the initial stages, these were extended to advanced Headquarters in most cases. In some instances single cable had to be used.

As soon as units became settled in position single wire circuits were made metallic.

Owing to the difficult nature of the ground and the fact that Brigades advanced across the extensive wire and trench system, nearly all lines had to be laid by drum barrow.

The wagons cable light were found to be very useful for taking up supplies of cable to points where they had to be carried forward by drum barrow parties.

Telephone & Sounder superimposed was used to Brigades when twisted cable was laid.

After extension on single lines became necessary D.3. and Fullerphone was employed.

It was found necessary to place lineman posts at very short intervals to ensure quick repairs to the very frequent breaks in lines.

Wireless

The efficiency of the Wireless system improved greatly in the later phases of the operations.

Difficulty was experienced at times from jamming and the encoding and decoding of long operation messages was found to be somewhat slow.

In the operations in front of Cambrai a large volume of traffic was dealt with by wireless between Division and Brigades when cable lines were frequently interrupted by heavy shell fire.

Loop Sets were used but did not give good results.

The distance of Battalion Headquarters from Brigades was usually greater than the efficient range for these Sets, very few men were trained in their use.

Power Buzzer & Amplifier

These Sets were used at MOEURES and in front of CAMBRAI and were of great service in badly shelled areas, they were carried forward by Headquarters Section and issued out to Brigades only when position of Headquarters became settled.

Casualties made it difficult to fully man these sets and the loop sets at the latter stage.

Pidgeons

Excellent results were obtained from pidgeons, Brigades were anxious to get as many birds as possible.

Visual

More use might have been made of visual, the chief difficulty was to find the personnel to operate visual stations and also maintain lines as Battalion and Brigade pool signallers became reduced in numbers.

Dispatch Riders

The Motor Cyclist D.R. system worked very efficiently throughout the operations.

After heavy rains the tracks that had to be used to Brigade Headquarters were very difficult to negotiate.

The necessity for supplementing the motor cycle D.R. with mounted orderlies was noted.

A relay system of D.R. and runner was necessary at times.

Transport

Representation has been made by R.A. Sigs for the replacement of the wagon G.S.R.E. by 2 wagons limbered R.E. or G.S.

A lighter vehicle is desirable for moving forward stores and apparatus to open the advanced office.

Two limbered vehicles are much more suitable for a series of moves than the one heavy vehicle which at present carries all the stores.

A Motor cycle & sidecar is recommended for Officer in charge R.A. Signals in lieu of the riding horse provided for him.

Equipment

The present scale of equipment was found to be satisfactory.

The possession of additional P.O. 44 Telephones would be an advantage when ~~Magneto~~ circuits are so frequently used.

The supply of an additional 6 of these instruments is recommended.

Signed A.S. Anguin
Major R.E.
O.C. Signals 52 Division.

6/10/18

Vol 7

Confidential.

War Diary
52nd Divisional Signal Coy

From 1st October 1918
to 31st October 1918.

Volume XLI with appendices 1 to 7.

[Stamp: 52ND (LOWLAND) DIVISIONAL SIGNAL COMPANY]

Army Form C. 2118

WAR DIARY
or
INTELLIGENCE SUMMARY
(Erase heading not required.)

Instructions regarding War Diaries and Intelligence Summaries are contained in F. S. Regs., Part II. and the Staff Manual respectively. Title Pages will be prepared in manuscript.

Place	Date	Hour	Summary of Events and Information	Remarks and references to Appendices
QUEANT	1916 Oct. 2	1800	Advanced Div Hqrs moved to CANTAING MILL. The Div. relieved the 63rd Div. Existing communications were taken over but required modification, as 63rd Div Hqrs were at CANTAING VILLAGE. Four pairs of cable were laid from MILL to VILLAGE. 155 and 157 Bdes on the line both Hqrs at MARLIÈRE FARM. A test point was established just east of CANTAING.	
	3		Rear Div. Hqrs moved to GRAINCOURT, where one telephone was installed. A single line of cable was laid from there to CANTAING MILL	
CANTAING MILL	4		155 Bde attacked FAUBOURG DE PARIS of CAMBRAI. by night. A normal station was established near Div Hqrs but was not used by troops in front.	
	5		Road east of CANTAING heavily shelled causing many faults in lines. An additional test point was established further forward (ANNEX.) where a line was laid to them. 155 Bde came out of line and moved to	APP. 1.
	6		Diagram of communications is appended. Div. Hqrs moved to VAULX VRAUCOURT. Communications at CANTAING were handed over to relieving division, 57th.	
VAULX VRAUCOURT	7	1700	Coy entrained at VAULX VRAUCOURT Station.	

Army Form C. 2118

WAR DIARY
or
INTELLIGENCE SUMMARY
(Erase heading not required.)

Instructions regarding War Diaries and Intelligence Summaries are contained in F.S. Regs., Part II. and the Staff Manual respectively. Title Pages will be prepared in manuscript.

Place	Date	Hour	Summary of Events and Information	Remarks and references to Appendices
	1918 Oct.			
TINCQUES	8	0200	Coy detrained at 0200 and marched to Willets in LE CAUROY. Bdes were in Willets at (155 Bde) MAZIÈRES, (156) IZEL EZ HAMEAU, (154) GRAND ROULECOURT. M.G. Battalion at HUVIN HUEVIGNEUL. Communication to Bdes, etc. was obtained over permanent lines allotted by Corps.	
LE CAUROY	9		Division in GHQ reserve. Company refitting and training.	
	19	1500	Div. Hqrs moved to Château D'ACQ by road. 155 Bde moved to LIEVIN, 156 to CHATEAU DE LA HAIE, 157 to MONT ST ELOI. Bdes were connected to Div. by lines arranged by Corps.	
CHATEAU D'ACQ	20	1300	Div. Hqrs moved to HENIN LIETARD by road. 155 Bde moved to FOUQUIERES 156 to BILLY MONTIGNY, 157 to HENIN LIETARD. Cables were laid to connect Bdes to Div. Diagram of lines is appended	APP. 2
HENIN LIETARD	21		All three Bdes moved forward. Lines were laid to their new positions. The lines to their old positions were reeled up. Diagram is appended	APP. 3
	22	1200	Div. Hqrs moved to CHATEAU BLANCHE MAISON by road. Diagram of lines is appended	APP. 4

WAR DIARY
INTELLIGENCE SUMMARY

(Erase heading not required.)

Army Form C. 2118

Instructions regarding War Diaries and Intelligence Summaries are contained in F.S. Regs., Part II. and the Staff Manual respectively. Title Pages will be prepared in manuscript.

Place	Date	Hour	Summary of Events and Information	Remarks and references to Appendices
CHATEAU BLANCHE MAISON	1914 Oct. 24		Div¹ H.Qrs moved to FLINES by road. Cables were laid connecting Bdes in new positions to Div. Diagram is appended	APP. 5
FLINES.	25		Div¹ N/T station was opened. to work to Corps.	
"	27		15th Bde moved to LECELLES and 157 to LANDAS. Both Bdes were connected by existing lines to 12th Div at SAMEON.	
"	28		15th Bde went into the line and came directly under the 12th Div. 157 moved into support at LECELLES & 155 to reserve at LANDAS	
"	29	1600	Div¹ H.Qrs moved to SAMEON. and relieved 12th Div. All existing lines etc were taken over. A party of 30 cavalry from 4th Hussars were attached for duty. 7 were sent to 15th Bde in the line, to be used as dispatch riders, etc.	
SAMEON	30		Diagrams of communications established from Div to Bdes and from 15th Bde forward are appended	APP. 6. APP. 7.
"	31		Classes for instruction in Power Buzzer worker were started at Div H.Qrs for Infantry signallers	

Army Form C. 2118.

WAR DIARY
or
INTELLIGENCE SUMMARY.
(Erase heading not required.)

Instructions regarding War Diaries and Intelligence Summaries are contained in F. S. Regs., Part II. and the Staff Manual respectively. Title pages will be prepared in manuscript.

Hour, Date, Place	Summary of Events and Information	Remarks and References to Appendices
1918. Oct. SAMEON	During the month. 15 men went to hospital sick 4 " " " " wounded 2 " " were sent to base 6 " rejoined from hospital 13 " were received as reinforcements from base.	

H.G. Copestake Capt.
for Major R.E. (T.)
O.C. Low. Div. Sig. Coy.

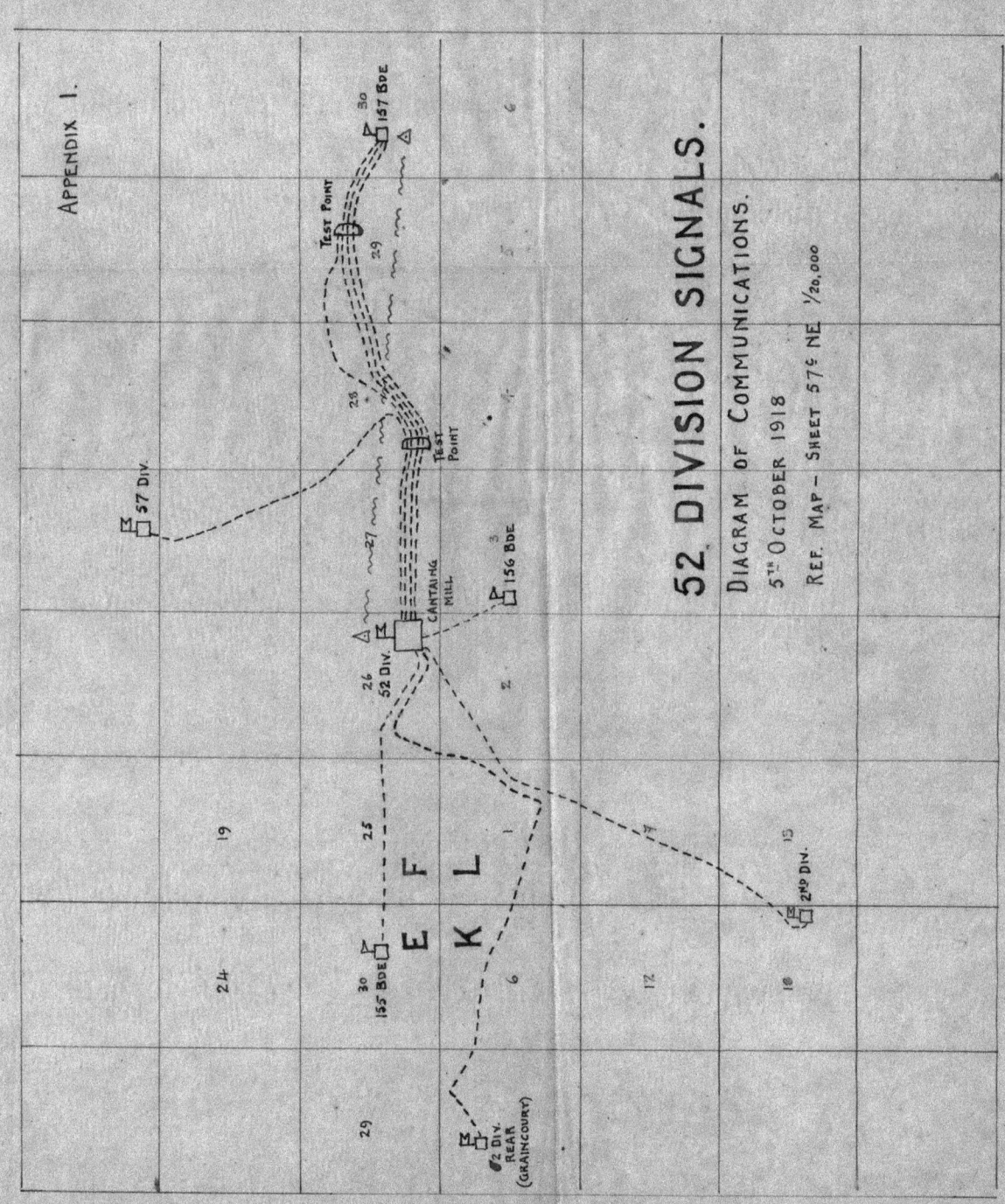

52 DIVISION SIGNALS — DIAGRAM OF COMMUNICATIONS.
20TH OCT. 1918. REF. MAP — SHEET 44A. 1/40,000.

APPENDIX 2.

		13	19	25	31
		18	24	30	HENIN-LIETARD 36 52 DIV.
				157 BDE 29	O P
				28	5
	FOUQUIERES 155 BDE	27 BILLY-MONTIGNY	33	34	4
	156 BDE		32	3	U V
				2	6
					1

52 DIVISION SIGNALS — DIAGRAM OF COMMUNICATIONS.

APPENDIX 3.

21st OCT. 1918.   REF. MAP — SHEET 44A 1/40,000.

52 DIVISION SIGNALS — DIAGRAM OF COMMUNICATIONS.   APPENDIX 4.

22ND OCT. 1918.   REF MAP — SHEET 44A 1/40,000.

HENIN-LIETARD

CCT PUT THRO ON GERMAN CANNEAU

52 DIV. ARTY.

COURCELLES 155 BDE.

CHAT⁴ BLANCHE MAISON. 52 DIV.

156 BDE.

AUBY

FLERS

157 BDE. CHAT⁴ FLERS

O P Q
U V W

52 DIVISION SIGNALS — DIAGRAM OF COMMUNICATIONS. APPENDIX 5.

24TH OCT. 1918. REF. MAP — SHEETS 44A & 44, 1/40,000

(Communications diagram showing grid references with the following annotated locations:)

- COUTICHES — 156 BDE
- FLINES — 157 BDE
- 52 DIV.
- 52 M.G. BATT'N
- RACHES
- 155 BDE — CHAT'U PLAISANT
- 52 DIV. ARTY — FRAIS MARAIS

Station symbols: Q R / W X (left side); R M / X S (right side)

APPENDIX 6

Sheet 44

Route Diagram 52nd Divn Comm.ns
30th Oct. 1918

1:40,000

APPENDIX 7.

156 INF BRIGADE: DIAGRAM OF COMMUNICATIONS
30ᵗʰ OCT. 1918. REF. MAP SHEET 44. 1/40,000.

NOTE: 277 BDE RFA. THRO' 63 BDE RFA.
      w/T to 52 DIV.

- 4 R.S. (J27 A 57)
- A BATTY 63 BDE RFA
- 7.S.R. (J27 D 77)
- 156 BDE (J27 D 24)
- 63ᴿᴰ BDE RFA
- 7 R.S. (J29 C 96)
- W. COY 7 R.S.
- B COY 52 M.G. BATT'N

NOT TO SCALE

War Diary

52nd Lowland Divisional Signal Coy.

From 1st November 1918
To 30th November 1918.

VOLUME XLII

with Appendices 1.6-5

WAR DIARY
or
INTELLIGENCE SUMMARY
(Erase heading not required.)

Army Form C. 2118.

Hour, Date, Place	Summary of Events and Information	Remarks and References to Appendices
1916		
Nov.1 SAMEON		
1600	157 Bde Hqrs moved to RUMEGIES. A cable line was laid to them direct from Div Signal Office. A diagram of communication is appended	APPENDIX 1.
0600 " 5	157 Bde Hqrs moved to MINERAL SPRINGS at P17 B67.	
" 5	155 Bde Hqrs moved to RUMEGIES. 157 Bde took over the existing communications of the Bde of the 8th Div whom they relieved.	
" 6	A diagram of communications is appended. The enemy withdrew on the Div front, and was followed up by 156 and 157 Bdes. A cable wagon was attached to each of these Bdes and moved forward with them laying cable. A forward Div Wire was opened at MAIRIE DE NIVELLE to transmit messages if lines got too long and to act as a test point.	APPENDIX 2
" 8	A D.S. Officer was attached at this office. 157 Bde eventually got out of touch by wire, owing to their moving. Nevertheless we still signals got to front by working	

WAR DIARY
or
INTELLIGENCE SUMMARY.
(Erase heading not required.)

Army Form C. 2118.

Hour, Date, Place	Summary of Events and Information	Remarks and References to Appendices
1918		
1600 Nov. 9 SAMEON	Div. Hqrs moved to MONT DU PERUWELZ.	
" 10 MONT DU PERUWELZ	Div. Hqrs moved to SIRAULT. It was found impossible to maintain communication by wire between MONT DU PERUWELZ and SIRAULT, owing to the Belgian inhabitants cutting out pieces of cable out of the line. Two were caught red-handed and arrested. 156 Bde were now at SIRAULT and 156 and 157 Bdes both in the neighbourhood of VACRESSE. All were connected by cable to Div. Signal Office.	
" 11 SIRAULT	155 Bde moved to JURBISE, and 156 Bde to HERCHIES in preparation for attack at 0700. A cable was laid from SIRAULT thro' HERCHIES to JURBISE with a tee off to VACRESSE.	
1100 " 11 "	Hostilities ceased. In the rapid advance from SAMEON to SIRAULT all the Company's motor transport got into difficulties, owing to the bad state of the roads and the bridges having been demolished by the enemy.	

WAR DIARY
or
INTELLIGENCE SUMMARY.
(Erase heading not required.)

Army Form C. 2118.

Hour, Date, Place		Summary of Events and Information	Remarks and References to Appendices
1918.			
Nov. 11	SIRAULT	The only transport that arrived to time was horse-drawn.	
" 15	"	The Div Signal School, which had been running since 19th Sept was broken up. The classification of the candidates had not been completed. It was arranged that this should be carried out at the Base.	
1500 " 18	"	Div Hqrs moved to NIMY north of MONS.	
" 16	"	A Diagram of communications is appended	
" 18	NIMY	Owing to the move of Div Hqrs a new cable line was laid from NIMY to JURBISE. This was mixed above the ground by attaching to trees along road.	APPENDIX 3.
0400 " 19	"	157 Bde Hqrs moved to Chateau at LA VERRERIE. A cable line was laid to connect them to NIMY.	
1000 " 19	"	Div Artillery Hqrs moved to J30 C37. They were connected by cable to NIMY.	
" 22	"	A diagram of communications as at this date is appended	APPENDIX 4

Army Form C. 2118.

WAR DIARY
or
INTELLIGENCE SUMMARY.
(Erase heading not required.)

Instructions regarding War Diaries and Intelligence Summaries are contained in F. S. Regs., Part II. and the Staff Manual respectively. Title pages will be prepared in manuscript.

Hour, Date, Place	Summary of Events and Information	Remarks and References to Appendices
1916		
28 Nov. NIMY	The lines to 155 Bde and Div Artillery were put through existing permanent routes and cable to these places relaid up.	
1500 28 Nov. NIMY	152 Bde moved to LOMBISE. A pair on a permanent route was repaired and put through to them.	
30 Nov. "	A diagram of communications as at this date is attached	APPENDIX 5
	During the month the following casualties occurred:— Lieut Hanbury to hospital sick on 7th " " " from " on 23rd 2 men went to hospital wounded 22 men " " " sick 2 men were sent to Base 2 reinforcements joined from hospital 19 do do from base.	

J.G.Christie Capt.
for
Major R.E. (?)
O.C. Lon. Div. Sig. Coy.

APPENDIX I.

52ND DIVISION SIGNALS — DIAGRAM OF COMMUNICATIONS —

1ST NOV. 1918   REF MAP - SHEET 44

52ND DIVISION SIGNALS – DIAGRAM OF COMMUNICATIONS

APPENDIX 2
REF. MAP SHEET 44
6TH NOV. 1918

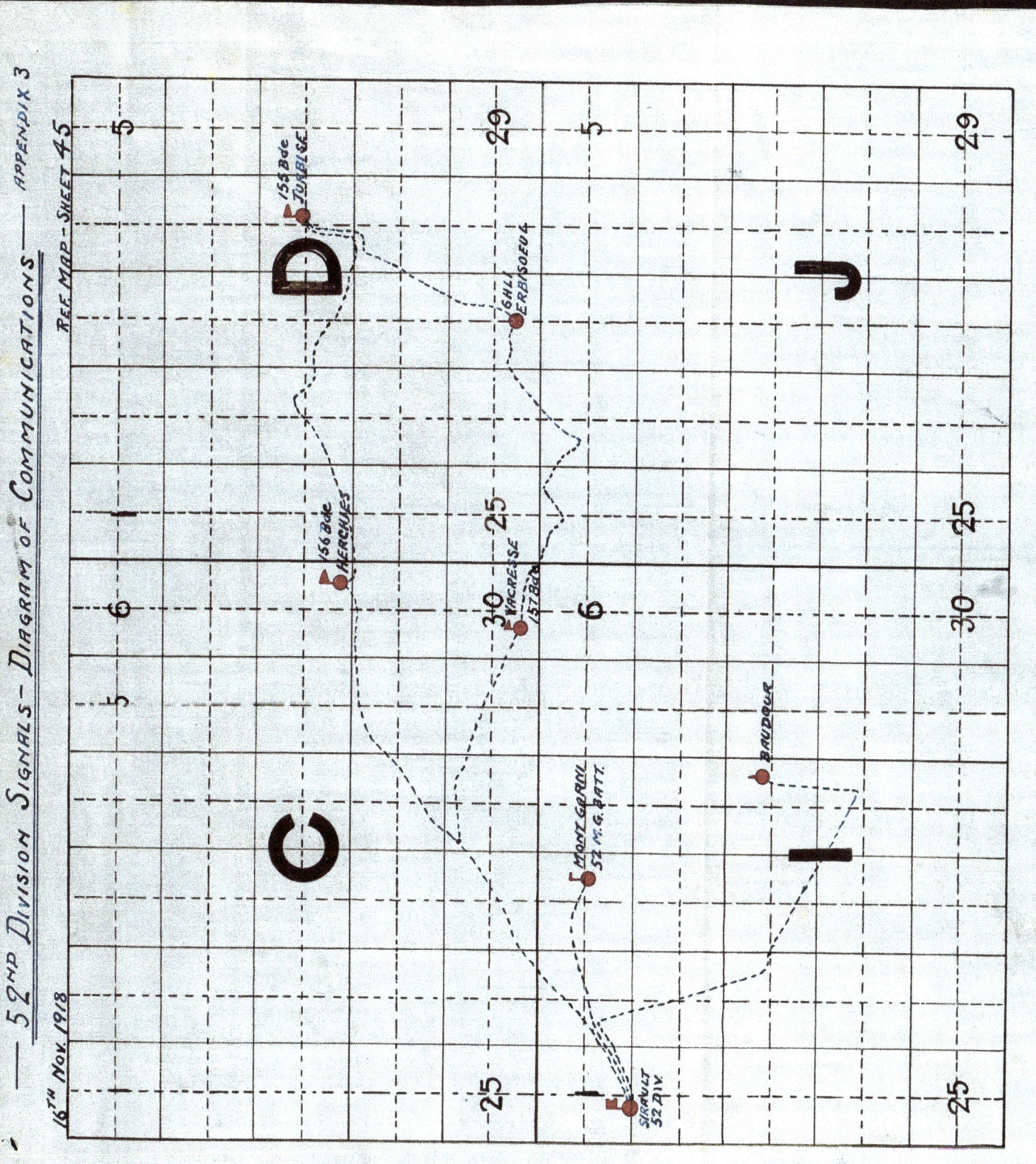

— 52ND DIVISION SIGNALS — DIAGRAM OF COMMUNICATIONS — APPENDIX 4

22ND NOV. 1918

REF. MAP - SHEET 45

- 155 Bde. TURBISE
- ERBAUT
- 56 Bde. R.F.A.
- 156 Bde. HERCHIES
- 9 Bde R.F.A. MAGRESSE
- 157 Bde. LA VERRERIE
- NIMY, 52 DIV.
- 52 D.A.H.Q.
- 52 M.G.BATT. BAUDOUR

C D E
I J K

52ND DIVISION SIGNALS – DIAGRAM OF COMMUNICATIONS

APPENDIX 5

30TH NOV. 1918

REF MAPS SHEETS 38 & 45

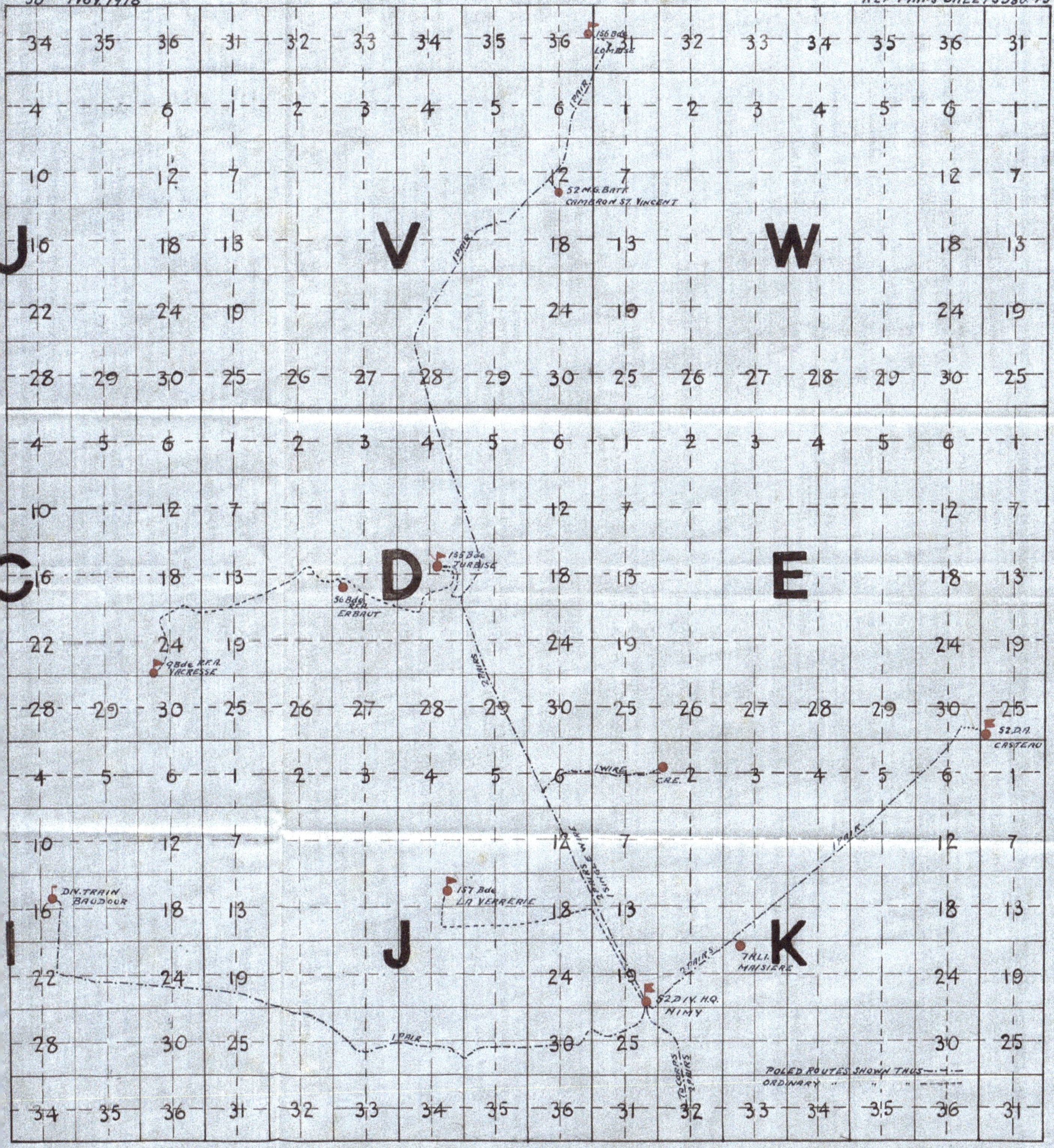
V
W
D
E
J
K
156 Bde
LOMBISE
1 PAIR
52 M.G. BATT.
CAMBRON ST. VINCENT
155 Bde
TURBISE
56 Bde R.F.A.
ERBAUT
9 Bde R.F.A.
VACRESSE
2 PAIRS
1 WIRE
C.R.E.
52 D.A.
CASTEAU
DIV. TRAIN
BAUDOUR
157 Bde
LA VERRERIE
1 PAIR
7 H.L.I.
MAISIERE
2 PAIRS
52 DIV. H.Q.
NIMY
TO CORPS 2 PAIRS
POLED ROUTES SHOWN THUS
ORDINARY " " "

Confidential

War Diary.

52nd (Lowland) Divisional Signal Coy.

from 1st December 1918 to 31st December 1918.

VOLUME XLIII.

Army Form C. 2118.

WAR DIARY
or
INTELLIGENCE SUMMARY.
(Erase heading not required.)

Instructions regarding War Diaries and Intelligence Summaries are contained in F. S. Regs., Part II. and the Staff Manual respectively. Title pages will be prepared in manuscript.

Hour, Date, Place	Summary of Events and Information	Remarks and References to Appendices
1918 Dec. 31 NIMY	During the month, the division was concentrated in positions occupied in November. There was no change in the Signal communications. Wireless stations were kept open at Ath, Mons and the three Infantry Bdes. In connection with the Army Education scheme, classes were started in the company in French, Mathematics, Applied Mechanics, Electricity and Magnetism. In the last named subject men from other units in the division attended. During the last fortnight, the work of preparing demobilization papers was carried on. 8 men were sent to hospital sick 5 " rejoined from hospital 14 " joined as reinforcements from Base No 418064 Sergt SUTHERLAND was awarded a bar to his M.M. 419052 2/Cpl DICK, R " " M.M.	

W/B Patrick Capt.
for
Major R.E. (T.)
O.C. Low. Div. Sig. Coy.

Confidential

War Diary

52nd (Lowland) Divisional Signal Coy.

from 1st January 1919 to 31st January 1919.

Volume XLIV.

Army Form C. 2118.

WAR DIARY
or
INTELLIGENCE SUMMARY.
(Erase heading not required.)

Instructions regarding War Diaries and Intelligence Summaries are contained in F. S. Regs., Part II. and the Staff Manual respectively. Title pages will be prepared in manuscript.

Hour, Date, Place	Summary of Events and Information	Remarks and References to Appendices
1919 Jan. 31 NMY	During the month of January, the division remained concentrated in positions occupied in December. There was no change in the Signal Communications. The classes in connection with the Education Scheme were continued. During the month Lieuts Johnson and Watson and 31 other ranks were demobilised. 8 men were sent to hospital sick 8 men rejoined from hospital 2 reinforcements were received from the base H G Capstake Capt. for OC NZ(C) Sig Coy.	

War Diary.

52nd (Lowland) Divisional Signal Coy.

From 1st Feb 1919 To 28th February 1919.

Volume XLV.

WAR DIARY
or
INTELLIGENCE SUMMARY.

Army Form C. 2118.

Hour, Date, Place	Summary of Events and Information	Remarks and References to Appendices
1919 Feb. 28 NIMY	During the month, the division remained concentrated in positions occupied in January. There was no change in the Signal communications. On 7th Feb., owing to so many men being demobilised, all the educational classes except those in "Telegraphy" and "Telephony" and "Mathematics" were discontinued. On 25th Feb., No.5 Section and the two Artillery Ble subsections were withdrawn and concentrated at D.H.Q. During the month, 112 O.R. were sent off for demobilisation. 39 O.R. were transferred to units in Armies of Occupation. 10 O.R. were sent to hospital sick. 5 O.R. rejoined from hospital. 13 horses were sent to the base.	

NGGpstah Capt
for Major R.E. (T.)
O.C. Low. Div. Sig. Coy.

52ND (LOWLAND)
DIVL. SIGNAL COY.

Vol 12

War Diary

52nd (Lowland) Divisional Signal Coy.

From 1st March 1919 To 31st March 1919.

Volume XLVI

Secret

Army Form C. 2118.

52ND (LOWLAND)
DIVL. SIGNAL COY.
R.E.

Date 31.3.19

WAR DIARY
or
INTELLIGENCE SUMMARY.
(Erase heading not required.)

Hour, Date, Place	Summary of Events and Information	Remarks and References to Appendices
1919		
1st March NIMY	Sapper HORNE was awarded the Military Medal published in XXII Corps Routine Orders of 28th Feb.	
9th " "	Lieut LAZARUS was transferred to Signal Subsection of 26th Army Bde R.G.A.	
19th " "	From 1st to 19th March, the units of the division remained in the stations occupied in Feb. On 19th concentration of cadres at SOIGNIES began. A signal office was opened at SOIGNIES. As Bde cadres moved they were connected by telephone to that office.	
25th " "	Div Hqrs moved to SOIGNIES. All educational classes finished during the month, the last of the horses were disposed of. 67 other ranks were sent for demobilization, 12 " " were transferred to units in the armies of occupation.	

J G Chisholm Capt/
O.C. 52nd Div. Sig. Coy.

WD 13

Confidential

War Diary

52nd (Lowland) Divisional Signal Coy. R.E.

from 1st April 1919. to 30th April 1919.

Volume XLVII

52ND (LOW.) DIVRL.
SIGNAL COY., R.E.

Army Form C. 2118.

WAR DIARY
or
INTELLIGENCE SUMMARY.
(Erase heading not required.)

Instructions regarding War Diaries and Intelligence Summaries are contained in F. S. Regs., Part II. and the Staff Manual respectively. Title pages will be prepared in manuscript.

52ND (LOW.) DIVNL. SIGNAL COY., R.E.

No. ....
Date. ....

Hour, Date, Place	Summary of Events and Information	Remarks and References to Appendices
1919		
1st April SOIGNIES	Demobilisation AFG 1098 for Hd Qrs & No1 Section signed by DADOS 52nd Division.	MSH
3 "	Major A.S. ANGWIN. DSO. MC. demobilised. – Capt H. GOODALL COPESTAKE assumed command.	MSH
4 "	Lt LEEVES transferred to Army of Rhine	MSH
8th "	2nd Lt. HAY joined from 11th Signal Coy.	MSH
8th "	Lt. R.B. HOVEY struck off Coy Strength & returns in U.K.	MSH
14 "	Capt. H. GOODALL COPESTAKE demobilised – Capt R.W. MACPHERSON M.C. assumed command.	MSH
17 "	Lt. J.M. KIDD transferred to No1 Area Clearing up Army	MSH
17 "	Cadre (4 ORs) of 9th Bde RFA Signal Sub Section transferred to H.Q. 9th Bde	MSH
18th "	Lt HAY demobilised	MSH
18th "	Lt. E. MADGWICK transferred to No4 Area Clearing up Army	MSH

Army Form C. 2118.

WAR DIARY
or
INTELLIGENCE SUMMARY.
(Erase heading not required.)

Instructions regarding War Diaries and Intelligence Summaries are contained in F. S. Regs., Part II. and the Staff Manual respectively. Title pages will be prepared in manuscript.

Hour, Date, Place	Summary of Events and Information	Remarks and References to Appendices
1919		
21st April SOIGNIES	Lt A MARSHALL demobilised	A504
	During the month 32 other ranks here sent for demobilisation	A504
	5 Other ranks here transferred to other units	A504
	1 Other rank to hospital.	A504

52ND (LOW.) DIVNL.
SIGNAL COY., R.E.

No.................
Date.................

R W Mayhew Capt RE
O.C. 52nd Div. Sig. Coy.

62ND (LOW) DIVNL.
SIGNAL COY, R.E.

War Diary

52nd Divnl Signal Coy R.E.

1st May 1919 to 31st May 1919.

Vol XLVIII

Army Form C. 2118.

WAR DIARY
or
INTELLIGENCE SUMMARY.
(Erase heading not required.)

Instructions regarding War Diaries and Intelligence Summaries are contained in F. S. Regs., Part II. and the Staff Manual respectively. Title pages will be prepared in manuscript.

52nd LO"(LAND)
DIV. SIG. CO'Y.
4 June 1919

Remarks and References to Appendices

Hour, Date, Place	Summary of Events and Information	
1919		
1st May Soignies	Location unchanged — Communication to MONS SUB AREA by telegraph. — Telephone to Local units & Telephone.	
2nd May "	Lieut Geo Bates joined for duty with Coms.	
5th May "	3 ton Lorry & Sunbeam car returned to Depot.	
9th May "	Lieut H.P Hardbury transferred to L Signals ROUEN	
27th May "	Lieut Jno Kerr rejoined from RHINE ARMY.	
	During the month 76 other ranks were despatched to UK for demobilization 6 other ranks were transferred to other units.	

[signature] Lieut
for O.C. 52nd Div. Sig. Co'y

www.ingramcontent.com/pod-product-compliance
Lightning Source LLC
Chambersburg PA
CBHW081440160426
43193CB00013B/2338